RISE OF THE ROBOTS!

ROBOTS FIGHTING WARS

WILL ROBOTS TAKE OVER THE WORLD?

Louise Spilsbury

CHERITON
CHILDREN'S BOOKS

Published in 2024 by **Cheriton Children's Books**
1 Bank Drive West, Shrewsbury, Shropshire, SY3 9DJ, UK

© 2024 Cheriton Children's Books

First Edition

Author: Louise Spilsbury
Designer: Paul Myerscough
Editor: Jennifer Sanderson
Proofreader: Katie Dicker

Picture credits: Cover: Shutterstock/Corona Borealis Studio (top), Shutterstock/Dark Geometry (bottom). Inside: p1: Shutterstock/Keith Tarrier, p4: Shutterstock/Pavel Chagochkin, p5: Shutterstock/Digital Storm, p6: Wikimedia Commons/Oshkosh Defense, p7: Shutterstock/Getmilitaryphotos, pp8-9: Shutterstock/Felipe Teixeira, p8l: Shutterstock/PressLab, p8r: Carnegie Mellon University, p9: US Air Force, p10: Shutterstock/Getmilitaryphotos, p11: Hstar Technologies/US Army, p12: Shutterstock/Gorodenkoff, p13: Shutterstock/Wirestock Creators, p14: Shutterstock/Dark Geometry, p15: Wikimedia Commons/PFC Rhita Daniel, p16: US Navy/MCS 2nd Class Joshua Scott, p17: US DOD, p18: Wikimedia Commons/Outisnn, p19: Shutterstock/BPTU, p20: Shutterstock/Artem Grebenyuk, p21: Wikimedia Commons/US Air Force/Bobbi Zapka, pp22-23: Shutterstock/Gorodenkoff, p22l: United States Marine Corps, p23: Shutterstock/Theodor Negru, p24: Wikimedia Commons/Uavtek, p25: Shutterstock/Frame Stock Footage, p26: Shutterstock/Dan Simonsen, p27: Wikimedia Commons/US Army, p28: Wikimedia Commons/Lt. Col. Leslie Pratt, p29b: Shutterstock/Kutsenko Volodymyr, p29t: Wikimedia Commons/Ministry of Defence of Ukraine, p30b: Shutterstock/Michal Zduniak, p30t: Wikimedia Commons/Erişim, p32b: Shutterstock/Aleksandar Malivuk, p32t: NASA/Tony Landis, p33: Shutterstock/Keith Tarrier, p34: Shutterstock/Fotogrin, p35: Liquid Robotics, p36b: Shutterstock/Yasemin Yurtman Candemir, p36c: Saab Group, p37: Wikimedia Commons/National Museum of the US Navy, p38: Shutterstock/Kryvenok Anastasiia, p39: Alamy/Associated Press, p40: Shutterstock/Algol, p41: Shutterstock/Andrea Danti, p42: US Navy/John F Williams/Released, p43: Shutterstock/Gorodenkoff, p44: Shutterstock/Pavel Chagochkin, p45: Boston Dynamics.

All rights reserved. No part of this book may be reproduced in any form without permission from the publisher, except by a reviewer.

Printed in China

Please visit our website,
www.cheritonchildrensbooks.com
to see more of our high-quality books.

CONTENTS

Chapter 1 *Battle of the Bots* 4
Robot Takeover: Superpowered Bots 10

Chapter 2 *Small but Deadly* 12
Robot Takeover: Armed and Ready................ 14

Chapter 3 *Eyes in the Sky* 20
Robot Takeover: High-Tech Superspies 24

Chapter 4 *Bot Sky Wars* 26
Robot Takeover: Deadly Drones 30

Chapter 5 *Wars on Water* 34
Robot Takeover: Bot Battle Boats 40

Chapter 6 *Future Robot Soldiers* 42
Robot Takeover: The Ultimate Army 44

Glossary 46
Find Out More 47
Index and About the Author 48

Chapter 1

BATTLE OF THE BOTS

Imagine fighting an army of soldiers that never stops. The soldiers don't pause to eat or sleep. They cannot be reasoned with. They feel no sympathy, regret, or fear. If they are hit, they are patched up and sent straight back onto the battlefield. They have one mission and nothing can distract them. They just keep on going. Military robots are already in action and fighting wars. In the future, machines will fight more and more battles. Will robot armies one day take over the world?

BOTS OF ALL SIZES

In sci-fi movies, robotic soldiers are usually shown as fearsome humanoids. This means they look like humans, with a head, eyes, arms, and legs. Scientists around the world are working on robots like this, and there are some already in action. But most of the robots that fight wars today come in many different shapes and sizes, from tiny tanks to drones shaped like insects. The term "robot" means a machine that can be programmed to move, perform tasks, and gather information from its surroundings.

Could this be what all soldiers of the future look like?

ROBOTIC SOLDIERS ON DUTY

In war, robots take on many different military roles, from transportation and search and rescue to full attack.

Going to war is dangerous. Many service people are injured or lose their lives in the line of duty every year. Military **personnel** have to deal with a range of dangerous situations, from removing unexploded bombs to rescuing people from a town that has been invaded by armed enemy forces. The advantage of using robots is that humans do not need to put their lives at risk. And because robots are machines, they are less likely to make mistakes or get carried away by feelings such as anger and fear, which can cause a lapse of judgment in the heat of battle. Robots are also easily replaced, unlike humans.

In the future, more armies will use robotic soldiers to give them a competitive edge in battles.

BIG BOT DEBATE

Is It Right for Robots to Fight Wars?

Robots fighting wars is no longer science fiction or futuristic. It is real. At the moment, people program and control the robots that are used in war, even if from a distance. What if this changes in the future? Some people are concerned that military robots may become so advanced that they can make choices for themselves, and those choices may not be good ones. For example, they worry that because robots do not have emotions, they would not be able to show compassion to an enemy. Other people argue that this would be a good thing because it would make robots more effective warriors. Do you think robotic wars are a good or bad idea?

MIGHT IS RIGHT!

Some military jobs require brute force and serious strength. For such tasks, large military robots are useful. Some of these monster machines can plow through just about anything.

ROBOT ROLLOVER

The largest unmanned ground vehicles (UGVs) are built for action and survival in the line of fire. Heavy-duty UGVs are covered in strengthened steel so they can survive explosions. They can also ride over anything, including tricky, uneven **terrain**, on sets of wheels or on caterpillar tracks. Caterpillar tracks have a ridged belt of metal that moves around large wheels. The ridges dig into snow, sand, and mud to provide grip.

SUPERBIG BOTS

A UGV can weigh many tons. The multiple wheels or caterpillar tracks spread this weight over a large area so that the heavyweight robot does not sink. They also help keep it stable. A UGV's route is usually controlled by a soldier with an operator control unit (OCU) at a safe distance away or from inside an armored vehicle. The OCU is like a remote controller.

SOLDIER SAVERS

When an enemy is at large, troops need extra protection. One UGV task is to carry troops safely into the battlefield so they are fresh to fight. TerraMax is a troop-carrying UGV. It is a huge, autonomous truck, which means it drives itself. Smart tech allows TerraMax to steer, brake, and speed up or slow down on its own. It follows routes sent from an OCU linked to **GPS** maps.

> TerraMax UGVs can travel in convoys, or lines of vehicles all traveling together, behind manned Marine Corps vehicles.

TERRAMAX TECH

TerraMax is bristling with cameras and **sensors** to spot enemies or unexpected obstacles. Using this information, operators can decide to change route, **deploy** weaponry, or retreat (turn back) to keep the soldiers the bot is carrying safe.

Using robotic vehicles such as TerraMax to transport troops across the battlefield reduces the danger to soldiers and saves lives.

ROBOTS RISING UP!

Tank units can make the difference in winning a ground war. But tank crews face incredible danger from enemy tank fire. Enter armed robotic vehicles, or ARVs! ARVs such as the Russian Marker robot are powerful enough to carry a wide range of weapons. These can include anti-tank missiles and cannons. Marker also carries sensors that allow it to move autonomously over terrain and to spot targets to destroy. One Marker can detect other Markers, so they can move together in a formation toward the enemy.

NO NO-GO ZONES

The toughest all-terrain robots can survive the challenges of almost any battlefield. They keep going in places that many other vehicles would need to stop. Tree stumps, brush, rocky riverbeds, and bombed-out buildings are minor obstacles for these mighty UGVs.

CRUSHER, THE BOT

Crusher by name and crusher by nature! Crusher is a six-wheeled all-terrain bot that can carry equipment, supplies, and injured soldiers over the roughest ground without anyone inside feeling a single bump. Crusher weighs around 6.5 tons (6 mt) and can travel at up to 25 miles per hour (40 kph), even over rocky terrain. The front of this robotic vehicle is reinforced, or strengthened, so that Crusher can just knock aside obstacles as it hurtles forward across the ground.

CRUSHER CLIMBER

Crusher's power and grippy wheels enable it to climb over 4-foot (1.2 m) walls and glide up steep slopes. It has an extra springy **suspension** that allows each wheel to travel 30 inches (76 cm) independently.

Crusher's ability to carry precious **cargo** anywhere makes it an ideal medevac (medical evacuation) vehicle for injured soldiers.

ARTS is a 6.5-ton (6 mt) vehicle that can be transformed into a multipurpose tool such as a forklift or a mine remover.

IN THE FRAME

Crusher has a high-strength aluminum and titanium frame, with a thick steel plate beneath. This plate protects Crusher's contents from any blows that hard objects, such as rocks, may cause.

DEADLY DOZER

You might not consider a bulldozer to be a military tool but think again. The Armored Combat Engineer Robot (ACER) is a bulletproof beast of a robot with multiple capabilities. This means it can do many different jobs. ACER can have a steel scoop fitted at the front. The scoop can easily push aside **debris** to clear routes through a battlefield. ACER can also be fitted with a grabbing and cutting device, which can chop up large debris into smaller chunks. It can also take on the role of firefighter when fitted with a foam-firing nozzle.

DRIVERLESS DIGGER

The All-Purpose Remote Transport System (ARTS) is like Crusher's smaller cousin. ARTS is also multifunctional. Fit brushcutters, and it can clear paths through thick bushes so that soldiers can see what they are doing while searching for **mines**. Attach a gripping arm, and ARTS can handle suspicious objects that could explode. Operators can safely view the objects via video feed from cameras on the robot. It can also have a minesweeper fitted. This device detects buried mines and explodes them while humans remain a safe distance away.

ROBOT TAKEOVER: SUPERPOWERED BOTS

We are a long way from full-on robotic wars but robots are gradually taking over many aspects of military conflict. Imagine being a soldier on the ground, trudging miles a day while carrying heavy kit including weapons and their bullets, rations, water, and communications equipment. How exhausted do you think you would be? After hours of marching, would you be able to react quickly if the enemy attacked? The Small Multipurpose Equipment Transport, or S-MET, could.

Taking the Load

The US military uses S-METs to do a very important job. They are designed to carry 1,000 pounds (454 kg) of equipment—that's nine soldiers' worth of gear. S-METs allow each member of an **infantry** squad to carry far less kit themselves, so they don't tire as quickly and so they can move faster. Soldiers are trained to cover long distances, so S-METs have the battery power to travel 60 miles (97 km) over three days. S-METs also act as a charging point: Soldiers rely on life-saving equipment such as night-vision goggles and radios that need charging after repeated use.

Designed for Action

S-METs have four pairs of mini-monster-truck tires to ride over the battlefield. These are powered by a **hybrid** electric engine that charges itself as it moves. It has a **flatbed** at the back, with room inside for heavy gear. There is also room on top to move extra loads, such as injured soldiers. Even though the S-MET is quite large, a soldier can operate it with a single-handed OCU. That means the soldier always has one hand free to reach for their weapon or other important kit when they need to.

When ground troops enter danger zones, robots can be sent ahead to carry out **reconnaissance** to help protect human lives.

The Battlefield Extraction-Assist Robot (BEAR) is designed to rescue soldiers from the battlefield.

Robotic Leaders

Running out of water or bullets on the front line could be disastrous. When infantry are in the battle zone, their safety may depend on getting more supplies. S-METs are designed to move in smart convoys. They autonomously follow a lead truck driven by a soldier, matching the route and speed of the leader. In the future, the lead vehicle could be another S-MET, operated at a distance by a soldier. Together, they can keep a company of infantry in action until the battle is won.

BIG BOT DEBATE

Are Superpowered Bots a Help or a Hindrance?

Some people think that S-METs and other robotic mules are a great idea. They argue that S-METs allow each member of an infantry squad to carry far less kit themselves, so they don't tire as easily and they can move faster. In the battle zone, a soldier's safety can depend on getting more supplies, which S-METs can deliver safely and easily. Other people think these bots are a hazard. They say that S-METs are designed to move in smart convoys. They autonomously follow a lead truck driven by a soldier, matching the route and speed of the leader. That means they could travel in the wrong direction and deliver supplies to the enemy. Do you think S-METs are useful or do you believe they could cost battles and lives?

11

Chapter 2

SMALL BUT DEADLY

Many of the most useful robots in the military are small in size. Some are capable of deadly force and can be highly dangerous. But many others work with army personnel to carry out a wide range of tasks on missions where their small size is a distinct advantage.

MILITARY MACHINES

Small UGVs can get right into the action on a battlefield. They can clear unexploded bombs and make minefields safe to cross. They can also take up a forward position to secretly observe the enemy. Operators a safe distance away may control the bots by tablet computer or laptop OCU. They take advantage of sensors on the bots to assess risks, from counting the size of the enemy force to identifying substances that could be harmful to the soldiers.

ROBOTS RISING UP!

The deadliest small robots have killer cargo. Remote Weapon Stations such as PROTECTOR or ADDER are units combining sensors and weapons that can be fitted to UGVs and many other types of military vehicle. These can automatically aim and fire at targets. The stations are partly controlled by an OCU and are partly autonomous. For example, operators instruct the station on how to recognize the enemy. Then the station uses onboard cameras to scan the area. If it spots a target, it uses a **laser rangefinder** to calculate its distance. Then, if it is close enough, it fires.

UGVs can silently observe enemy soldiers and their movements.

Dutch soldiers are being trained to operate this THeMIS UGV, which is armed with a machine gun.

BUILT TO SURVIVE

Small UGVs are very adaptable. They are tough enough to survive drops and explosions. Many are sealed units that are amphibious. This means that they can drive on land and through water, such as deep puddles, rivers, and swamps.

SNEAKY BOTS

Smaller UGVs do not always have the power supply needed to march long distances into battle. They may need recharging or refueling more often than bigger UGVs. However, they are much easier to carry near to the action by soldiers, on jeeps, or even on larger UGVs. The most commonly used robots are small, flat designs with caterpillar tracks. That's so they can sneak through small gaps and into tight spaces on the battlefield, and travel over any surface, hard or soft.

13

ROBOT TAKEOVER: ARMED AND READY

Robots are beginning to have a role on the battlefield, boosting the firepower of the military. The ground troops of the future could have autonomous mini-tanks moving at their side with awesome defensive powers. The Modular Advanced Armed Robotic System (MAARS) is a small, powerful UGV that is a comrade-in-arms any soldier would want by their side.

Safer Soldiers

MAARS was designed to help keep soldiers in forward locations as safe as possible. It can operate day and night owing to its video cameras, which are sensitive to light and also to heat given off by living things. Onboard sensors can detect movement, too. The cameras, sensors, and arms are mounted on a tower that can swivel all the way around. That helps MAARS detect and react to threats from any angle.

Stop the Fight

Shooting to kill should be an absolute last resort in any conflict. When MAARS encounters the enemy and the mission is to deter, or discourage, them from fighting, it has some less-harmful options it can use. These include speakers that can play messages warning about the dangers of fighting. They also include special eye-safe lasers with beams that can dazzle and confuse the enemy.

The Last Resort

When there is no option other than to fight, MAARS can let rip. It has multiple **grenade** launchers. Some are loaded with harmful, but not deadly, options. These include **tear gas**, lights, and smoke. If these fail, the last resort is to unleash high-explosive grenades and to fire its machine gun.

If robotic soldiers of the future are trained to kill, they should do so only as a last resort.

These soldiers are testing the capabilities of MAARS. This little bot is a best friend to troops navigating a battlefield.

BIG BOT DEBATE

Surveillance Bot

MAARS was designed specifically to carry out **surveillance** and target-finding missions, for example, looking out for enemy targets, and routes military should take or attack from, to be more successful in a conflict.

Enemy-Proof Robot

Imagine if the enemy suddenly controlled this lethal robot. MAARS has a trick up its sleeve to prevent this from happening. It can operate only when it receives coded instructions from the OCUs of its own forces. It can go into sleep mode for up to a week or it can be on active duty for 12 hours. Only after receiving the correctly coded command is it ready to go.

Do UGV Troops Keep Soldiers Safe or Put Them at Risk?

Some people think that UGVs such as MAARS are a great development for ground troops. They argue that MAARS can detect and react to threats from any angle, day or night, so it keeps troops safer. Other people fear the UGV could suddenly be controlled by the enemy and start firing on its own troops. However, designers of MAARS argue that it can operate only when it receives instructions, making it a reliable bot. Do you think the UGV keeps soldiers safer or do you think it may put them at even greater risk?

TALON is a small-but-tough robot that can carry out a wide range of military missions.

ROBOTS ON DUTY

Soldiers are trained to do important jobs that may be too dangerous for civilians, or ordinary people not in the military. They are a vital part of the response to many crises, from natural disasters to hostage situations. But robots can also be on duty for these tasks, rather than endangering human lives.

TALENTED TALON

TALON is one of the most widely used UGVs. This little robot has a mechanical arm that can be fitted with many different tools for various tasks, such as gripping and picking up things. TALON has X-ray equipment that can see through solid materials to check if there's an explosive device inside. The robot also has wire cutters that can snip cables on a device to stop it exploding.

BOT SURVIVOR

TALON moves on caterpillar tracks and it is very stable. If it falls over because it tries to pick up something too heavy, it can right itself. It simply releases the object and pushes itself up. TALON is also tough. It can survive after being blown up and can return to work once sensitive parts such as cameras and sensors are replaced.

ROBOT TEAMWORK

MATILDA is a small, slow robot ideal for search-and-rescue missions. Its job is to look for survivors in places too dangerous for soldiers to enter, such as a factory where an accident has spilled harmful substances. MATILDA can be fitted with cameras to see the survivors, and microphones to hear them. This robot can get inside small spaces but also carries a smaller robot called MARV, which can fit into the tightest gaps. It can be used to search under rubble after a building has collapsed. If MATILDA finds survivors, rescue missions can begin.

ROBOTS RISING UP!

The Vision 60 (V60) has four legs and is shaped like a headless dog. It can climb hills and stairs, run, and swim. Its head has sensors to "see" where it is going. But if these stop working, this remarkable robo-dog can return to base using only GPS signals. It is ideal as a patrol robot, for example watching out for enemies crossing borders. The V60 is generally controlled using an OCU but in an Australian experiment, the operator used their brainwaves: A sensor on the operator's head detected their brainwaves that were then turned into command signals for the robo-dog.

MATILDA can get inside buildings, climb stairs, and navigate through piles of rubble.

CARRY-ON COMMANDOS

Imagine a portable robotic army that could fit in carry-on bags. The most portable military UGVs can do just that! Although small in size, they can carry out big-impact missions.

ROBOT IN A BACKPACK

Soldiers often scan the land ahead, wondering, "Is it safe to walk along this path? Is that an old cooking pot or is it a bomb?" They are right to consider every action—in battle, there are dangers everywhere. In some military zones, improvised explosive devices (IEDs) are a major hazard for soldiers. Enemy forces disguise and hide these bombs to try to harm soldiers. For example, in a conflict in Afghanistan, US troops came upon IEDs hidden in networks of caves where enemy troops were hiding. Luckily, the US troops were carrying PackBots in backbacks. These are small, tracked robots fitted with cameras and a gripper arm.

PACKBOTS PATROL

PackBots can be made ready for use within a couple of minutes. Soldiers watch on their OCU screens as the PackBots move forward. They direct the robots toward suspicious objects and they instruct the robotic arm to lift or move objects so IEDs are visible. PackBots can also drive over a bomb to explode it. After all, exploding a robot is far better than killing a human.

Soldiers use PackBots in enemy-held buildings to search for enemy fighters.

Recon Scout is a robot that can be thrown into action, so it's known as a throwbot. It is the shape of a small dumbbell and weighs just 1.2 pounds (540 g). Soldiers might throw it into a **compound** where prisoners are kept, into a tunnel, or through the window of a building. Recon Scout is tough enough to survive the landing. Then it moves along on its two wheels. An onboard **infrared** video camera sends live feed back to the operator even when it is pitch black all around. This reconnaissance information is used by commanders to decide on what course of action to take next.

ROBOTS RISING UP!

Military forces could soon be using robotic tunnelers. Tunnels underground are a way for armies to move around in secret, for example to resupply troops or spy on the enemy. Pipe-worm is a robot inspired by earthworms. It moves forward in a pipe by inflating small bags filled with air at the front. This helps the bot grip the sides of a tunnel. It then inflates a bag at the back to push its front forward. In the future, larger versions of Pipe-worm may be able to dig tunnels themselves.

Recon Scout can send live footage of any activity it discovers during missions.

Chapter 3

EYES IN THE SKY

In war, knowledge is power. And there is no better way to know what your enemy is up to than by keeping a close eye on them. Small UGVs can get close to enemies on the ground but most reconnaissance happens from the sky, high above the action. Flying can be dangerous, so most eyes in the sky are mounted on unmanned aerial vehicles (UAVs), commonly known as drones.

FLYING AND SPYING

Military drones fly over enemy territory in search of enemy troops and camps. Drones are also used to find injured soldiers in search-and-rescue operations. Some drones are small and a little like model airplanes. It takes only one person to carry, launch, and control them. They can fly short distances at moderate altitudes, or high above sea level. The drones are difficult for enemies to spot. Other drones are the size and scale of small fighter aircraft. They can fly high on patrol over long distances. Without the extra weight of crew, they use less fuel to fly farther than similar-sized airplanes. The flight of a drone is controlled partly by a pilot using an OCU on the ground or in another vehicle, and partly autonomously by onboard computers.

> Drones in the sky can track the movement of enemy tanks on the ground without being seen.

The big, bad Global Hawk can take off at night and stay in the air during daylight hours before landing again the next evening.

HAWK HUNTER

The top-level reconnaissance drone used across the world today is the Global Hawk. This beast is the length of a school bus with a **wingspan** nearly three times as long. It is made from aluminum, fiberglass, and other materials that give it high strength with low weight. Global Hawk flies using a powerful engine. It can fly higher than the altitude at which commercial airliners fly, for well over a day and non-stop, before it needs refueling. The airplane's pilot monitors Global Hawk's flight from a ground operating station using a computer mouse.

SUPERSPY BOT

The bulge on the bottom of Global Hawk houses its reconnaissance technology. It has special **radar** equipment to spy on the ground, through sandstorms, clouds, and rain. Cameras can take detailed pictures of an area tens of thousands of square miles in a single day. Inside the bulge on its top is a **satellite** communications antenna. Global Hawk sends information such as reconnaissance photos to the ground operating station via satellites. It receives command data, or information, from Earth via that same satellite link.

EASY MOVERS

Soldiers on the ground are always on the move. They need an UAV that can be transported easily so they can take it with them and use it wherever their patrol goes.

MEET A ROBOT NAMED RAVEN

The Raven is a lightweight drone that looks like a small plane. It comes in kit form: It is made up of three different pieces that can fit into a backpack. An operator can put the pieces together so the Raven is ready to be thrown up into the air, like a paper plane, within minutes. Raven can find its way autonomously using GPS technology. Operators can also control its route from the ground. Raven can take off and land just about anywhere, making it a perfect drone for soldiers on the move.

EYES ON THE ENEMY

Raven has cameras that send detailed, real-time images and information back to the operator. Infrared cameras take pictures at night too. They detect heat energy and show colored shapes of things that give off heat on screen. This can show troops where enemy soldiers are hiding or gathering at night.

If the enemy spots Raven, operators can press a button that tells it to return to its launch point immediately.

BLACK EAGLES

Like Ravens, Black Eagle drones are named for a deadly bird of prey, but these drones look more like small helicopters than planes. The advantage of helicopter-style **rotor** wings is that Black Eagles can take off and land vertically. They can also hover in mid air. Black Eagle drones can work for up to 50 minutes in hover mode and up to 1.5 hours in flight mode. That means they can spy on vehicles, ships, and soldiers, gathering information about what enemy forces are up to and where they are going.

MASTER MOVERS

Black Eagles are special because their rotors mean they can go to places where plane-style drones like Raven cannot. For example, Black Eagles can fly straight down into narrow-sided valleys in mountainous areas. Then they can simply fly straight up and out again.

The rotors on the Black Eagle mean it can pause, stop, and hover at any point during its flight mission—like the helicopter above.

ROBOTS RISING UP!

Like many other surveillance drones, the Black Eagle can also be fitted with technology that helps it detect and identify enemy targets. They can carry small missiles and bombs that could be used to strike ground targets.

ROBOT TAKEOVER: HIGH-TECH SUPERSPIES

Will it be impossible for any of us to hide from the prying eyes of robots one day in the future? Will robots be able to watch us and find out all about us without us even knowing they are there? Perhaps, because new, tiny spy drones known as Bugs can sneak into areas without being seen and snoop on enemies. They are small enough to hover around, finding out all they need to know, and then buzz off before being spotted.

Bot Bugs

The Bug drone is made for surveillance and is one of the most advanced military robots in the world. This lightweight UAV is the size of a smartphone and can fit in the palm of a hand. It's fully autonomous and can be easily launched from the hand, the ground, or a moving vehicle. The Bug drone has a range of about 1.2 miles (2 km) and a battery life of about 40 minutes. Inspired by the dragonfly, which has four wings to hold the insect steady in the air, the Bug drone has four powerful rotors that can keep it flying, even in very strong winds.

Secret Snooper

The Bug drone has a flattened shape and camouflage colors that make it difficult to spot. When flying at a certain altitude, it looks just like another bird in the sky, and no one would even notice it. The difference is that this flying bot carries a high-tech camera. The pictures it takes are beamed back to troops via its antennae. Bug drones can send vital tactical information about what is around the corner or over the next hill, in even the wildest weather.

Soldiers can use Bug drones to spy on targets up to 1.2 miles (2 km) away.

Minute Machines

In the future, Bug drones will be even smaller—as tiny as bumblebees! They will also soon have infrared-detection capability. That means a Bug drone could fly undetected into a room at night through a small gap, and locate people in the dark by detecting the heat their bodies give off. This drone could photograph, record, and fire on enemies.

Could Bug drones help soldiers by spotting enemies long before they reach their targets? Or could they instead spy on us in the future, listening to all our conversations?

BIG BOT DEBATE

Are High-Tech Superspies Useful or an Invasion of Privacy?

Some people say that Bug drones are a step forward in surveillance. They say that Bug drones will become even smaller and have an infrared detection capability too, so they can locate people in the dark. This would be helpful in finding terrorists or other criminals. Other people argue that Bug drones might soon be spying on everyone, whether they are a threat or not. They say that Bug drones invade our privacy and that we will be constantly watched. Do you think Bugs are useful or a threat to our privacy?

Chapter 4

BOT SKY WARS

In the heart of the battle, strike planes scramble into aerial combat. They drop bombs and fire missiles, weakening the enemy and allowing their forces to advance. In the past, success relied on a pilot's split-second decisions, skill, and bravery. But now, combat drones are getting into the action. Unmanned combat aerial vehicles (UCAVs) are a deadlier step up from UAVs. They are the future of aerial warfare.

BUILT FOR BATTLE

In modern military combat, aircraft pilots face many dangers. They may experience **G-forces** that press on the body when flying fast or be shot at by enemy planes or by sophisticated weapons on the ground. UCAVs have no onboard pilot who could get sick from G-forces or be injured or killed in action. And they can fly and maneuver as fast, and carry just as many weapons, as most regular strike aircraft.

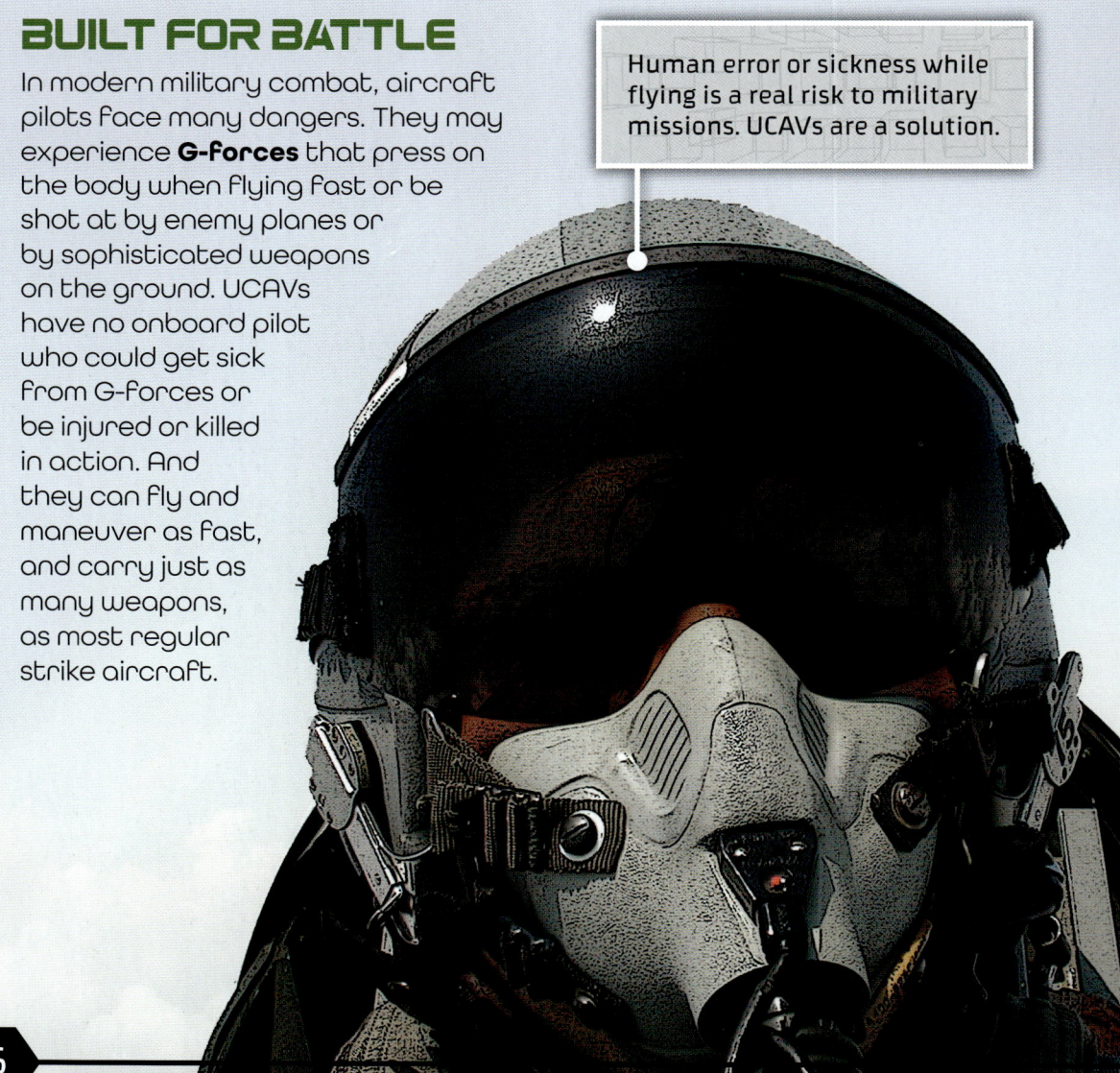

Human error or sickness while flying is a real risk to military missions. UCAVs are a solution.

The Gray Eagle UCAV can fly for 25 hours and carry multiple powerful **payloads**, including deadly missiles.

MILITARY MASTERMINDS

A pilot of a regular aircraft does not need to always steer or change speed or course or engine power. Instead, they can rely on technology called autopilot to help, so they don't get tired out on long flights. But the pilot is still in control of the aircraft. Modern UCAVs are almost fully autonomous. The new autopilot is the **artificial intelligence (AI)** in the computers of these drones. With programming, a UCAV can fly a complete mission from start to finish alone, including making lethal attacks on targets. Regular pilots need lengthy training and are expensive to hire, so using UCAVs can save air forces money.

ROBOTS RISING UP!

Imagine flying into combat with a drone at your side: a wingman that could fly in formation, distract the enemy, and even take a hit for you. A new breed of UCAV is built for just that. It's an uncrewed drone that can help protect the lives of pilots in crewed aircraft. And it is far better to have a drone damaged or destroyed than a hugely expensive modern fighter jet.

Reaper can strike an enemy target with extreme precision from a mile high!

DRONE DANGER

Some of the most battle-hardened UCAVs are already on duty in many conflicts around the world. Defense by drones is real and a vital part of tactical success for today's military operations.

AIR FORCE ACTION

The MQ-9A Reaper is a hunter-killer UCAV made by General Atomics. There are around 300 of these beasts flying for the US Air Force and many more in action in other countries. Reaper carries laser-guided air-to-ground missiles. These missiles fire at targets on the ground, which are lit up by light shone from another aircraft or drone, high above the action.

UNSTOPPABLE BOT

The Reaper is a propeller-driven drone with a 69-foot (28 m) wingspan. The engine is built for endurance, which means lasting a long time. Reaper can fly for more than 20 hours at a time, although this reduces to around 12 hours if it is carrying weapons. Two crew members in a ground station control the drone via instructions sent through satellites in space. The pilot commands the mission and an aircrew member operates sensors on the drone and guides the weapons to their targets.

LONG AND LETHAL

A Bayraktar TB2 drone costs around one-sixth of a Reaper. It does not travel as quickly and can carry one-tenth of the weapon weight but it can fly for just as long. And the TB2 is just as lethal. It is shaped like a small aircraft and has a digital flight control system with autonomous takeoff, cruise, land, and park. The TB2 follows routes using GPS but also has an inbuilt navigation system that can figure out its position and send it home if GPS fails.

The Bayraktar TB2 is a flat, gray UCAV that hits targets using its laser-guided bombs with great precision.

ROBOTS RISING UP!

The TB2 became famous during the early months of the war between Ukraine and Russia, which began in 2022. Bombing missions against Russian targets such as tanks, rocket launchers, and guns using TB2s helped Ukrainian troops advance. TB2s also acted as **decoys** when other missiles attacked Russian military ships. There was even a popular song about the drone!

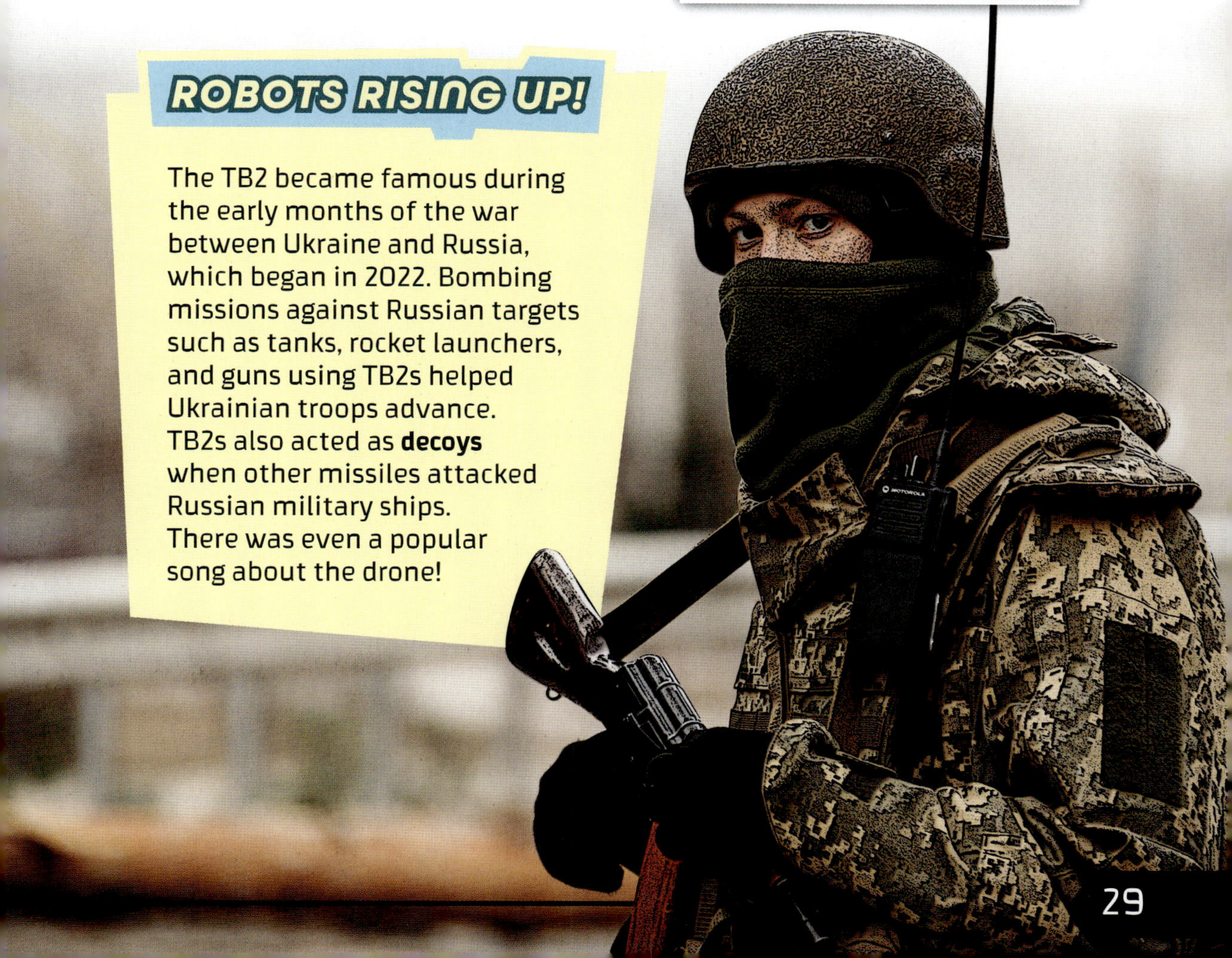

ROBOT TAKEOVER: DEADLY DRONES

In the not-too-distant future, aerial battles will be fought using combat drones. And one of the first will likely be the Kızılelma (which means red apple). This remarkable drone made by the Turkish company Baykar promises capabilities beyond those of many crewed aircraft.

Into Battle

Kızılelma is a jet-powered UCAV. It can take off from a very short, ramped runway, such as that on a small **aircraft carrier**. The drone does not need the helping hand of a slingshot launch to make it airborne. It can quickly reach its cruising speed of around 450 miles per hour (724 kph) and it can operate at heights of up to 30,000 feet (9,144 m). Kızılelma flies at around 6 miles (9.6 km) high and carries enough fuel to operate for 5 hours.

Bot Workaround

Fighter aircraft need to be highly maneuverable to chase the enemy at high speeds. But changing direction suddenly can cause aircraft to stall or lose lift from the wings. Kızılelma gets around this by having small stabilizers in front and above the main wings. These add extra lift and help the drone to keep flying if it stalls.

Sneaky Robot

Kızılelma is designed for stealth. Its jagged shape gives it a low radar cross-section (RCS). That means enemy radar cannot locate it as easily as they can detect aircraft with long wings or a less jagged shape. This drone has a state-of-the-art radar system. It can steer **radio waves** in different directions to detect approaching enemy craft and find targets. But the system also sends out the waves at different speeds. This makes it harder for the enemy to identify Kızılelma radar while it is in use. Enemies cannot jam, or block, Kızılelma's radar.

Kızılelma has air-to-air missiles to shoot down enemy drones, and missiles to destroy enemy ground radar.

BIG BOT DEBATE

Are Deadly Drones Helpful or a Danger to Armed Forces?

Some people think deadly drones will be fighting the aerial battles of the future. They argue that the high-tech radar and design allows Kızılelma to chase an enemy plane as acrobatically as most human pilots. It can carry more than 1 ton (0.9 mt) of firepower to destroy enemy radar and drones, making it safer for manned aircraft to join the battle. Other people think that deadly drones are a danger to their own forces. They fear that the radar could fail or the drone could fly into a manned aircraft while dodging attack at speed. They say that this type of technology is too new to be battle-proven. Do you think deadly drones will help us win wars or do you believe they are a danger to us?

Bomb and Blast

Kızılelma can carry well over 1 ton (0.9 mt) of firepower. Bombs in its internal weapon compartments include bunker busters. These are powerful enough to blast through hardened underground enemy shelters. Other weapons are carried on the underside of its 32-feet- (10 m) wide wings.

BOOMERANG BOT

The Phantom Ray looks like a boomerang with a bump in the middle. This hunter-killer drone has a 50-foot (15 m) wingspan and can carry nearly 2.2 tons (2 mt) of weaponry, from bombs to missiles. Its missions include bombing guns on the ground that could fire at their aircraft, seek-and-destroy assignments, and reconnaissance.

PUSHING AHEAD

Many lethal UCAVs of the future could share the same design: the flying wing. It has no tail and the large wings are blended into the body of the drone. The beauty of this design is that there is less **drag** than on conventional aircraft shapes. This means it uses less fuel.

DIAMOND DRONE

The experimental or X-class 47 drone is a diamond-shaped flying wing. It is designed for bombing missions in dangerous environments in which crewed aircraft would be under real threat. The drone takes off and lands from aircraft carriers. Its small wings fold up, so it takes up less space on a ship when it is not in use. The X-47 can stay in the air for longer than some drones because it can be refueled from airborne fuel carriers.

Soldiers in a control room plan missions, guide, and navigate Phantom Ray (shown above) in the air.

GOD OF THUNDER

The Taranis gets its name from the most fearsome of Celtic gods. This drone is so stealthy that it can hide from enemy detection. This is because of its very low RCS shape and a special coating on its wings. Taranis is designed to fly missions autonomously. Its sophisticated computer stores mission plans, allowing it to take off and fly on its own. A human pilot can control the Taranis from the ground but this is really only as a backup if the drone's systems fail to work.

LETHAL WEAPON

A new Indian UCAV called Ghatak, which means lethal, is deadly in battle. This drone can take off, navigate, complete a mission, and land again autonomously. It has a bank of control sensors that are capable of detecting visible and infrared light. Infrared light given off by objects can be detected when it is pitch black or cloudy. This allows Ghatak's onboard computer to calculate the drone's location, what is around it, and where the target is, day or night.

Taranis can reach speeds of over 700 miles per hour (1,126 kph).

Chapter 5

WARS ON WATER

As well as fish, whales, and other ocean wildlife, there are a number of military robots swimming below the ocean surface and floating along on the waves. These bots are designed for surveillance and to clear the waters of deadly mines. Some are also used to hunt, target, and sink enemy vessels.

DIRTY AND DANGEROUS!

Some of the naval robots that move and work underwater do three-dimensional (3D) work that can be dull, dirty, and dangerous!

These bots are like the grunts of the naval forces and they do important work, for example, they can be used to inspect the **hull** of a ship to see if it is damaged. They can also repair damage or replace worn-out parts underwater. They usually have long arms that can bend and lift. These arms can be fitted with tools such as rotating wire, nylon brushes, and water-jets for cleaning, or tools such as simple bars, hooks, and knives.

SPYING AT SEA

At a distance, a saildrone might be mistaken for a stiff windsurfer! In fact, naval saildrones are ocean robots that carry out another vital military job: surveillance. The Saildrone Explorer is an unmanned surface vehicle (USV) that is 23 feet (7 m) long and 16 feet (4.8 m) tall. Its huge wing catches the wind to help move it forward.

Underwater repair work can be dangerous for humans. Using a robot to carry out difficult and hazardous tasks is far less risky.

SOLAR-POWERED SPY

A rudder beneath the Saildrone Explorer controls its direction. The wing angle can be adjusted to ensure it catches enough wind to move. This hard-working robot can travel autonomously through wind and waves for up to 12 months. It has solar panels that provide the power for onboard cameras and sensors, which collect data above and below the sea surface to build a full picture of the ocean around it.

Another autonomous robot, the Wave Glider, gathers ocean data using onboard computers and sensors.

ROBOTS RISING UP!

Sending sailors out on patrol is a risk. If they come across enemy activity, they could be injured or killed. In the future, it is likely that the oceans will be full of robotic explorers carrying out sneaky surveillance. Even if a robot is dismantled, this information alone suggests a hostile force. Learning about a risk of attacks without harming humans is definitely a good thing.

MINE HUNTERS

Sea mines are often known as "weapons that wait." They can be chained to the ocean floor to explode on impact or float just beneath the surface, ready to blow up when a ship passes by. These deadly exploding devices are fairly cheap to make and place in waters around the world. Sea mines sink ships and injure and kill people, so the robots that detect and dispose of mines save lives.

UNDERWATER SEARCHER

Slicing through the water like a blade, the Knifefish searches for sea mines across the ocean. This unmanned underwater vehicle (UUV) moves quickly as soon as it is launched into the water from a naval ship at the surface. Its mission is to detect, locate, and identify mines at various depths, including on the ocean floor.

MINE MISSIONS

Knifefish uses a **sonar** system to find and track mines and minelike objects in the sea. Sonar systems send out sounds and then figure out where an object is by sensing the sound waves that bounce off the object. The information Knifefish collects is converted into digital data and transmitted to the naval ship waiting at the surface.

This Sea Wasp scans the seabed in search of deadly mines that lie in the ocean.

Unlike human divers, UUVs are not affected by cold temperatures, murky water, sharks, or hunger.

SEEK AND DESTROY

The Remus 300 and similar new UUVs go one step farther. These torpedo-shaped drones have high-resolution side scan sonar that can survey large areas in a single mission. As well as helping navies find and identify sea mines, Remus 300 can also spot sunken ships and aircraft that have crashed into the ocean. This robot can be carried by two people, which means it can be easily launched from a small boat or a harbor wall. It can dive up to a maximum depth of 1,000 feet (305 m). Remus 300 can also be fitted with the weapons it needs to destroy sea mines that it locates.

ROBOTS RISING UP!

Plans are underway to create a swarm of robotic diver drones that can communicate with each other. A larger robotic ship will release a group of smaller autonomous underwater robots. They will work together to seek, identify, and destroy mines. For example, when a UUV spots a suspicious object, it can alert another UUV to check it before exploding it.

SUPER SUBMARINES

Navies around the world are quietly developing robotic submarines that can be controlled by onboard AI. Some of these submarines are designed for surveillance but they also have the potential to fire missiles. With onboard AI, this could mean these submarines might one day fire on a target without direct human control.

WORKING ALONE

Countries do not want to reveal their progress so a lot of new robotic submarine plans are top secret. The few details we do know suggest that new robotic submarines will use sensors and **algorithms** to carry out complex missions on their own. Small UUVs are launched from a torpedo tube on the side of a crewed submarine. Then they move around, exploring areas and using sonar to create images of the ocean around them. If the UUV finds an enemy submarine, it sends information back to the main submarine. If the enemy sub is a threat, it could light up the target with sonar so that crew on the main submarine can destroy it with torpedoes.

ROBOTS RISING UP!

In the future, UUVs could be sent out from crewed submarines on a mission to hunt and possibly destroy enemy submarines. They could be used to sink enemy targets on their own without a human having to take the final decision to fire a weapon.

Underwater robot drones can carry out important surveillance efficiently.

RISE OF THE ROBO-SHARK!

An underwater robot that looks like a small-but-fierce shark is also taking to the water. Known as Robo-Shark, this 6.5-feet- (2 m) long military drone looks scarily like the real thing when it is cruising through the ocean! Instead of having a propeller like many other submarine drones, Robo-Shark has a battery-powered tailfin. It swivels back and forth to move the robotic fish along at speeds of up to 11.5 miles per hour (18.5 kph).

SPY AND SHOOT

Robo-Shark moves quietly and is difficult to spot. It is equipped with an all-around obstacle avoidance system, so it doesn't bump into anything as it travels. Robo-Shark is designed for surveillance but also has the potential to fire weapons. It has room inside to add new tech and missiles that could be used for different missions.

> Robo-Shark doesn't have teeth and won't bite like a real shark, but it can hurt its enemies in other ways!

ROBOT TAKEOVER: BOT BATTLE BOATS

Imagine a naval ship with no humans on board firing missiles at enemy aircraft in the sky. Or a fleet of robotic ships that use AI instead of sailors to fight at sea. Navies around the world are testing large autonomous robotic ships. These could be an effective way to protect the seas while putting fewer sailors' lives at risk. But what if armed robot boats start to take over the oceans?

Large and Dangerous

These robotic ships are known as large unmanned surface vehicles (LUSVs). They will be about 200 to 300 feet (60 to 90 m) in length, which is roughly the size of a long sports car such as a Corvette. LUSVs will have AI that gives them the ability to identify other vessels they meet and to steer a safe course around them. They will be designed to be able to carry out a variety of missions, including carrying radar and sonar for surveillance so they can act as scouts for a main battle fleet. The idea is that they would go ahead of crewed ships to detect threats early.

Cruising for a Bruising!

These LUSVs will also be able to shoot at enemy ships or fire land-attack missiles. Each LUSV could be equipped with 16 to 32 missile-launching tubes. This is so that they could leave port on their own, stay out at sea for months at a time, and then return to port autonomously for repairs and checks, or to be refitted with more weapons. While cruising the open ocean, they would have the power to take on and attack enemy ships and submarines.

Uncrewed military ships, like the one shown in this artist's impression, could change the way wars are fought at sea.

In the future, could robotic submarines replace crewed submarines? Could they look for and take down enemy targets? If so, what safeguards might be put in place to prevent them making mistakes?

BIG BOT DEBATE

Even Bigger

There are bigger and badder robotic boats in the pipeline too. XLUUVs (extra-large unmanned underwater vehicles) are being built that are roughly the size of a subway car. XLUUVs could be used to secretly deliver sea mines that would be attached to the seabed. These could also carry a variety of payloads, such as antisubmarine torpedoes.

Are Bot Battle Boats Good or Bad?

Some people think robotic boats are the future for navies. They could patrol the seas for months at a time and have the power to take on and attack enemy ships and submarines. This would keep sailors out of harm's way. Other people think that these battle boats are an accident waiting to happen. They argue that the robots could make a mistake and fire on submarines in their own navy or submarines carrying nuclear missiles, which could start a deadly conflict. Do you think bot battle boats are a good or bad idea?

Chapter 6

FUTURE ROBOT SOLDIERS

Many people believe that soon robots that look like humans will be fighting the world's battles. Inventors have already developed robotic skeletons that human soldiers can wear to help them in battles and other dangerous situations, such as fighting fires. And **prototypes** for robotic soldiers that can run, jump, and fight like a human, only better, are already being tested.

ROBOTIC FIREFIGHTERS

When a missile hits a ship or submarine, it starts a fierce fire. The flames, smoke, and fumes spread quickly through a confined space and can bring devastation. The heat can be intense and very difficult for human firefighters to tackle. SAFFiR is short for Shipboard Autonomous Firefighting Robot. This bipedal, or two-legged, humanoid robot is designed to put out fires that break out on ships.

SAFFiR the firefighting robot has a powerful gripper designed to deal with the strong **kickback** applied from a hose during fire-blasting operations.

TAKING OUT FIRES

SAFFiR is made of waterproof and heatproof materials. Although the robot is still in the trial stages, it will hopefully be able to react quickly to fires and withstand much higher temperatures than a human. It will put out lethal fires to save human firefighters.

WARRIOR SUITS

In the future, will we see robotic combat suits that provide a soldier with superhuman powers? Military robotics experts are hoping to develop a Warrior Suit—a robotic exoskeleton. This is a suit soldiers wear over their uniform to increase their strength, agility, and stamina.

SUPERSTRONG SOLDIERS

The Warrior Suit would have a small computer, controllers, sensors, and motors to allow it to move with the soldier. It would increase a soldier's strength to help them lift and carry weapons or move obstacles out of their way. The exoskeleton would also have to be flexible so that soldiers could still run, crawl, and climb while wearing it.

ROBOTS RISING UP!

How do you make a metal exoskeleton that is light enough not to slow or tire a human soldier but that also carries all the sensors, batteries, and other gadgets it needs to be useful? And how do you link the wearer's brain with the exoskeleton computer to create rapid sensing, without which there would be a delay between the operator wanting to move and the actual movement? These are obstacles, certainly, but technology has already overcome many of them.

Around the world, engineers are working on robo-soldiers that will fight future battles.

ROBOT TAKEOVER: THE ULTIMATE ARMY

Robotic exoskeletons worn by soldiers may help armies in the future, and it may not be long before there really are humanoid robotic soldiers fighting our battles too. The humanoid robot Atlas can already run, do backflips, and leap like an athlete. It can also pick up and throw heavy objects and perform other complex moves.

Awesome Atlas

Atlas is a highly advanced humanoid robot. It is nearly 5 feet (1.5 m) tall and has 28 **hydraulic** joints, three onboard computers, and battery-powered electric motors to make it move. It walks on two legs like a human, leaving its hands free to lift, carry, and fire weapons. It can hold and carry objects such as boxes and crates, and it can use its hands and feet to climb and move through most spaces. Atlas has been able to pick up a heavy kit bag and run up stairs, jump between levels, and push a wooden box from a platform without losing balance. It can keep its balance when it is pushed and it will get straight up if it's knocked down.

Soldier in Training

Atlas is being put through its paces as designers try to perfect robots that can perform real, physically demanding jobs at a human speed or even faster. Atlas has articulated, or jointed, hands with sensors that are designed to use tools that only humans can currently handle. It has depth-finder sensors to detect its surroundings. Atlas is still in the development stage but one day could it, or robots like it, be programmed to follow orders on a battlefield? Robotic soldiers would be far less expensive than a human army and fewer human soldiers would be killed if robots like Atlas took their place.

Do you find it frightening or comforting that in the future, entire armies might be made up of robots?

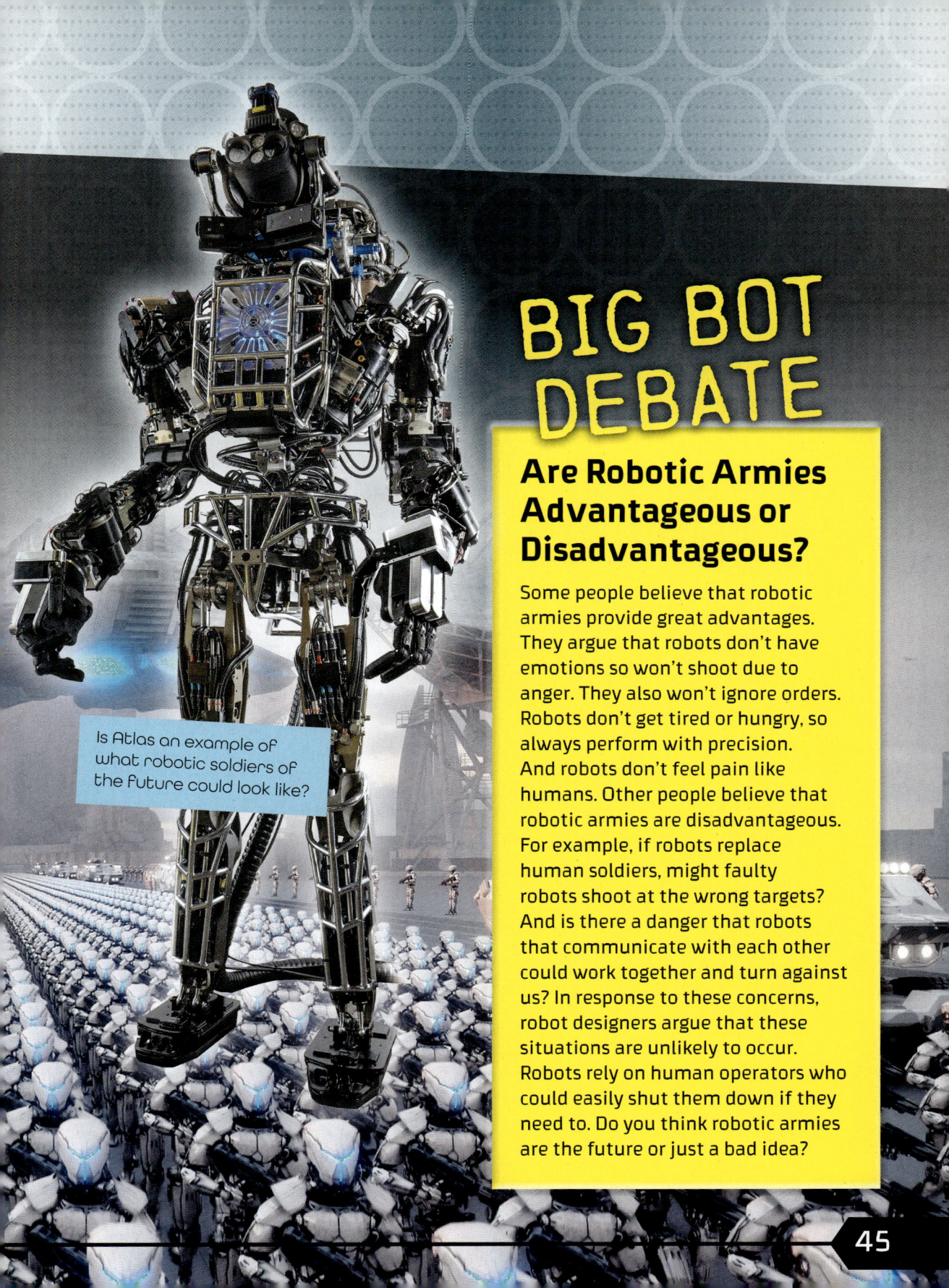

Is Atlas an example of what robotic soldiers of the future could look like?

BIG BOT DEBATE

Are Robotic Armies Advantageous or Disadvantageous?

Some people believe that robotic armies provide great advantages. They argue that robots don't have emotions so won't shoot due to anger. They also won't ignore orders. Robots don't get tired or hungry, so always perform with precision. And robots don't feel pain like humans. Other people believe that robotic armies are disadvantageous. For example, if robots replace human soldiers, might faulty robots shoot at the wrong targets? And is there a danger that robots that communicate with each other could work together and turn against us? In response to these concerns, robot designers argue that these situations are unlikely to occur. Robots rely on human operators who could easily shut them down if they need to. Do you think robotic armies are the future or just a bad idea?

GLOSSARY

aircraft carrier a military ship that has a large deck on which aircraft take off and land

algorithms sets of rules to be followed in calculations or other problem-solving operations

artificial intelligence (AI) the power of a machine to copy intelligent human behavior

cargo goods carried on a ship, aircraft, or motor vehicle

compound a cluster of buildings in an enclosure

debris pieces of garbage or remains

decoys objects that are designed to lure people into a trap or away from a target

deploy to move troops or equipment into position for military action

drag the force exerted by air or water that slows the movement of objects

flatbed an open, flat surface used for transporting cargo

G-forces forces that push on a person or object when they travel in space or very quickly through the air

GPS an acronym for Global Positioning System, a system of satellites that work together to provide exact locations on Earth

grenade a small bomb that can be thrown by hand or launched mechanically

hull the main body of a ship

hybrid powered by fuel and electricity

hydraulic using power from the pressure of water or another liquid to make a machine work

infantry soldiers who march and fight on foot

infrared describes rays of light that feel warm but cannot be seen

kickback a sudden, uncontrolled movement of a machine, tool, or other device

laser a very narrow beam of highly concentrated light

mines bombs placed on or just below the surface of the ground or in the water

payloads the total amount or weight of equipment and people that a vehicle can carry

personnel the people who are employed by a company or organization

prototypes the first working models of new inventions

radar a device that sends out radio waves to find out the position and speed of a moving object

radio waves forms of energy that can carry messages and information through the air

rangefinder a device for figuring out how far away an object is

reconnaissance studying or watching something to find out more about it

rotor a part of a machine that turns around a central point, such as a helicopter blade

satellite an electronic device placed in orbit around Earth to gather data

sensors devices that sense things such as heat or movement

sonar a system that uses sound waves to figure out the location, size, and movement of objects

surveillance keeping watch on or observing someone or something

suspension the system of springs and shock absorbers that supports a vehicle on its wheels

tear gas a gas that stings the eyes and fills them with tears

terrain an area of land with particular physical features, such as mountains

wingspan the length of an aircraft's wings, from tip to tip

FIND OUT MORE

BOOKS

Boutland, Craig. *New Generation Vehicles: Drones, Mine Clearance, and Bomb Disposal* (Military Machines in the War on Terrorism). Capstone Press, 2019.

Burrows, Terry. *Robots, Drones, and Radar: Electronics Go to War* (STEM on the Battlefield). Lerner Publishing Group, 2017.

Chandler, Matt. *Drones* (Military Science). Bellwether Media, 2022.

WEBSITES

Learn more about robots at:
https://kids.britannica.com/kids/article/robot/353723

Find out more about how robots and AI work at:
https://science.howstuffworks.com/robot6.htm

Are robots taking over armies? Read more at:
www.robotsscience.com/military/military-robots-history-types-use-and-how-it-work

Publisher's note to educators and parents:
All the websites featured above have been carefully reviewed to ensure that they are suitable for students. However, many websites change often, and we cannot guarantee that a site's future contents will continue to meet our high standards of educational value. Please be advised that students should be closely monitored whenever they access the Internet.

INDEX

amphibious 13
armed robotic vehicles (ARVs) 7, 14–15
artificial intelligence (AI) 27, 38, 40
autonomous 6, 7, 11, 12, 14, 20, 22, 24, 27, 29, 33, 34, 35, 37, 38, 40, 42

batteries 10, 13, 24, 39, 43, 44
bombs 5, 8, 9, 12, 16, 18, 23, 26, 29, 31, 32

cameras 7, 9, 12, 14, 16, 17, 18, 19, 21, 22, 24, 25, 33, 35
controllers/operators 5, 6, 7, 9, 10, 11, 12, 13, 15, 17, 18, 19, 20, 21, 22, 27, 28, 32, 33, 34, 43, 45

dangers 5, 7, 10, 12, 14, 15, 16, 17, 18, 20, 26, 28, 31, 32, 34, 40, 41, 42, 45
drones 4, 20–25, 26–33, 34–35, 36–37, 38, 39 (see also UAVs and UCAVs)

firefighting 9, 42–43
fuel 13, 20, 21, 30, 32

GPS 6, 17, 22, 29

hostage situations 16
humanoids 4, 42–45

lasers 12, 14, 28, 29

microphones 17
mines 9, 12, 34, 36, 37, 41

natural disasters 16
navigation 6, 11, 15, 17, 22, 29, 32, 33, 39, 40

privacy 25

radar 21, 30, 31, 33, 40
reconnaissance 10, 19, 20, 21, 32
remote weapon stations 12

satellite communication 6, 17, 21, 22, 28, 29
search and rescue 5, 17, 20
sensors 7, 12, 14, 16, 17, 28, 33, 35, 38, 43, 44
sonar 36, 37, 38, 40
speakers 14
submarine robots 38–39, 41
surveillance 15, 20, 23, 24, 25, 34, 35, 38, 39, 40

terrain 6, 7, 8, 9, 13
transportation 5, 6, 7, 10–11

unmanned aerial vehicles (UAVs) 20–25, 26 (see also drones and UCAVs)
unmanned combat aerial vehicles (UCAVs) 26–33
unmanned ground vehicles (UGVs) 6–11, 12–19, 20
unmanned surface vehicles (USVs) 34–35, 40
  large unmanned surface vehicles (LUSVs) 40
unmanned underwater vehicles (UUVs) 36–41
  extra-large unmanned underwater vehicles (XLUUVs) 41

weapons 7, 9, 10, 12, 13, 14, 23, 26, 27, 28, 29, 31, 32, 33, 34, 36, 37, 38, 39, 40, 41, 42, 43, 44

ABOUT THE AUTHOR

Louise Spilsbury is an award-winning children's book author who has written hundreds of books about science and technology. In writing and researching this book, she has discovered that robots are rising, revolutionizing our world, and paving the way for an awesome high-tech future!